Whatever the Weather

by Carmel Reilly

What Is the Weather?

The weather is what happens in the **atmosphere** each day.

What is the weather like today?

This weather is mild and sunny.

Weather is often mild. Mild weather can bring a gentle breeze.

Sometimes, weather can be extreme, too.

A severe storm brings heavy wind and rain.

Different locations, or places, have different weather. The land and sea can cause different weather.

Mountain Weather

It is cool in the mountains. It can be wet and windy, too.

Tall mountains can get substantial snowfalls.

Mountains get lots of precipitation. Precipitation is water that falls from the atmosphere. Rain and snow are kinds of precipitation.

A lot of rain falls on mountains.

Mountains have their own weather patterns. Wind and rain changes **direction** around a mountain.

Mountains can block sunlight.

Often, vegetation, or plants, cannot grow on mountain tops. It is too cold and rocky high up there.

Conditions in the mountains change quickly. Storms can come from any direction. A sunny day can turn icy cold.

Climbers must be ready for cold weather.

Desert Weather

Deserts are very dry. They get less than 250 mm of precipitation a year.

It is hard for vegetation to grow without water.

In the daytime, many deserts are hot. Conditions change after dark. Then, hot deserts can become very cold.

It is essential not to get too cold at night.

No rain may fall for months on end in a desert.

Sometimes, a severe storm hits.

A year's worth of rain can fall in one day.

Coastal deserts are near the sea. They get very little precipitation. Coastal deserts get water from sea fog and dew.

Fog has formed over the Atacama Desert.

Cold deserts are covered in snow and ice. However, they are very dry, too.

Antarctica gets a mere 150 mm of precipitation in a year.

Only some plants and animals live in deserts. They do not need much water.

These meerkats live in the hot desert.

Tropical Weather

Tropical locations are **humid** and wet. They lie around the middle part of the planet.

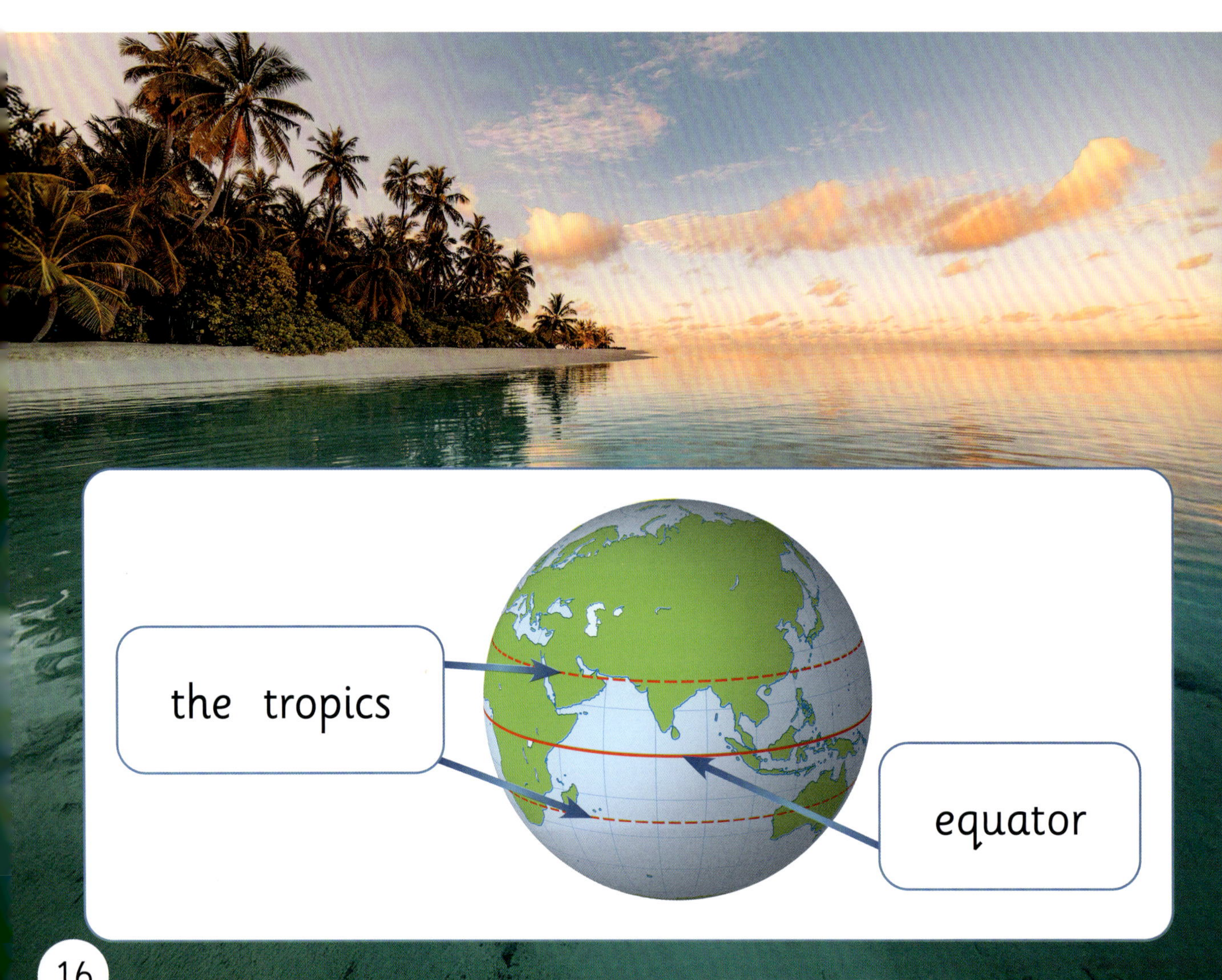

The tropics have two seasons. The wet season is hot and rainy. The dry season is hot and dry.

Substantial amounts of rain fall here in the wet season.

Tropical rainforests are humid. They get rain all year round. They have a lot of vegetation.

Trees are squeezed together in rainforests.

Many animals live in the tropics. There is a lot of food for them there.

A sloth peers around a tree.

Severe storms can hit the tropics. They can cause a lot of destruction. **Volunteers** often need to clean up after a tropical storm.

Parts of the tropics are in coastal locations. They have hot weather. They have cool sea breezes, too.

People love visiting tropical beaches.

Different Weather

Mountains, deserts and tropical locations have different weather.

Where do you live? What is the weather like?

Weather in different locations

Location	Weather
Mountains	cool with wind, rain and snow
Deserts	dry – hot or cold
Tropics	hot – wet or dry

Glossary

atmosphere: the air around and above us

conditions: what a place is like

direction: the way something is going

humid: hot and damp

volunteers: people who help others for free

Index